GW00579594

# *Feasts & Seasons*

# Spring

**Anthony Adams**
**Robert Leach**
**Roy Palmer**



**BLACKIE**

*BLACKIE & SON LTD*
*Bishopbriggs, Glasgow G64 2NZ*
*450 Edgware Road, London W2 1EG*


*First published 1978*

*ISBN 0 216 90397 1*



*Printed in Great Britain by Robert MacLehose & Co. Ltd*
*Printers to the University of Glasgow*

# Contents

# Acknowledgments

The authors and publishers are grateful for permission to use copyright material as follows:

J. M. Dent & Son Ltd for the recipe from *A Taste of Wales* by Theodora Fitzgibbon.

The Hamlyn Publishing Group Ltd for the extract from *The Encyclopedia of European Cooking,* edited by Musia Soper, published by Spring Books.

Curtis Brown Ltd on behalf of James Kirkup for the extract from *The Only Child,* by James Kirkup, published by Collins.

Oxford University Press for the extract from *The Lore and Language of Schoolchildren* by Iona and Peter Opie.

Edward Lowbury for "April the First" from *Daylight Astronomy* published by Chatto and Windus Ltd.

The Folklore Society for the extract from *British Calendar Customs.*

The Society of Authors as the literary representative of the Estate of A. E. Housman, and Jonathan Cape Ltd, publishers of A. E. Housman's *Collected Poems* for the extract from "Loveliest of trees, the cherry now".

Mrs R. Vaughan Williams for the tune by Ralph Vaughan Williams on page 40, from *English Folk Song: Some Conclusions* by Cecil Sharp, published by Heinemann.

The Estate of E. H. Shepard and Methuen and Co. Ltd for the extract from *Drawn from Memory* by E. H. Shepard.

E.F.D.S. Publications Ltd (Chappell & Co. Ltd) for "May Song" (Northants), collected by F. Hamer, copyright 1973.

The Trustees of the Hardy Estate and Macmillan, London and Basingstoke, for "Proud Songsters" from *Collected Poems* by Thomas Hardy.

*Illustrations*

The Mansell Collection pages, 1, 2, 3, 10, 33, 43 and 51.

A. F. Kersting page 5.

K. H. C. Taylor A.R.P.S. pages 14, 15, 34 and 35.

*Good Housekeeping* page 17.

Keystone Press Agency Ltd pages 24 and 25.

The Guardian and Manchester Evening News Ltd page 27.

Calder High School, Mytholmroyd page 31.

The Shakespeare Birthplace Trust page 37.

The British Library page 39.

G. N. Hopcraft page 48.

Curtis Brown Ltd on behalf of the Estate of E. H. Shepard page 49.

Whitbread & Co. Ltd page 52.

Watney Innkeepers and Michael Francis page 52.

G. N. Wright page 53.

Syndication International Ltd for the cover photograph.

*Music*

A special acknowledgment is due to Pat Palmer for the harmonization of songs and notes on their performance.

## The Youthful Spring

Now that the Winter's gone, the earth has lost
Her snow-white robes, and now no more the frost
Candies the grass, or calls an icy cream
Upon the silver lake, or crystal stream;

But the warm sun thaws the benumb'd earth,
And makes it tender; gives a second birth
To the dead swallow; wakes in hollow tree
The drowsy cuckoo, and the humble bee:

Now do a choir of chirping minstrels bring
In triumph to the world the youthful Spring.

Thomas Carew

# The Natural World

*The coming of spring means that the animals which have survived the rough winter are seen again. Those that have been in hibernation wake up, and birds return from migration. Spring flowers begin to push up – daffodils, Easter roses, none-so-pretty (London pride), sweet white violets and catkins. You might collect some of these to make a spring flowers arrangement.*

*You might also like to keep a nature diary for the months of spring in which you list the different animals, birds and flowers that you see, and make careful notes of where and when you spotted them. You could add what the weather was like each day. If this is done for several years it makes a very useful record and you can compare how quickly spring came in different years. You could keep the diary in the form of a large wall chart and include drawings or cut-out pictures of the various things that you see.*

## *Animals to Look For*

*Try to observe as many different animals as closely as you can and make notes about them – what they are doing when you see them, as well as their size, colour and so on. Here are some to begin with, but see what others you can find and make similar notes about them. You could illustrate your notes with drawings or photographs and make a large scrapbook of springtime animals.*

Squirrels

*Grey squirrels are much more common than red ones. They originally came from America: can you find out when they came to Britain? Squirrels usually seem very nervous and move quickly and with jerky movements. They will run up and down tree trunks and if they are frightened they sometimes make a sharp chattering sound.*

*Squirrels make nests for their young. Red squirrels often make more than one nest, and move their babies if they think there is danger where they are. They like to build in fir trees and particularly in pine trees. Grey squirrels prefer deciduous trees. A squirrel's nest has a dome-shaped roof and the entrance is through the side. Baby squirrels are born blind and with no fur.*

### Badgers

*Badgers live in sets made in banks or hillsides or woods. The sets are often quite complicated, having several entrances and several hollowed-out rooms.*

*Badgers move about carefully, usually at night. They eat insects, slugs, snails and baby birds or animals, as well as roots and bulbs. The babies are born blind and stay in the set with their mother for eight or nine weeks before they are able to go out alone.*

### Hares

*Sometimes in the spring you see hares leaping and bounding through the fields – they are mad "March hares".*

*Hares live in shallow hollows or other concealed places in the open – their homes are called "forms". They crouch in the form very still for hours.*

*The babies, known as "leverets", are kept in separate forms and the mother visits each of them in turn to feed them. After about a month they are strong enough to fend for themselves. Then they too will begin to race and jump and buck through the fields.*

## *Growing Things*

Beans

*Put a little water in the bottom of a jamjar. Roll up a piece of blotting paper and put it in the jar; when it unrolls inside the jar it will soak up the water. Put a broad bean seed between the blotting paper and the side of the jar. As the bean grows, record its progress – drawings, photographs and written descriptions are useful.*

Mustard and Cress

*Put a little water in the bottom of a plate. Place a piece of blotting paper over it. Sprinkle mustard and cress seed over the blotting paper. As the mustard and cress grows, record its progress.*

Carrot Top

*Cut off the top of a carrot. Place it with the leaves uppermost in a saucer with a little water in it. Record what happens to the carrot.*

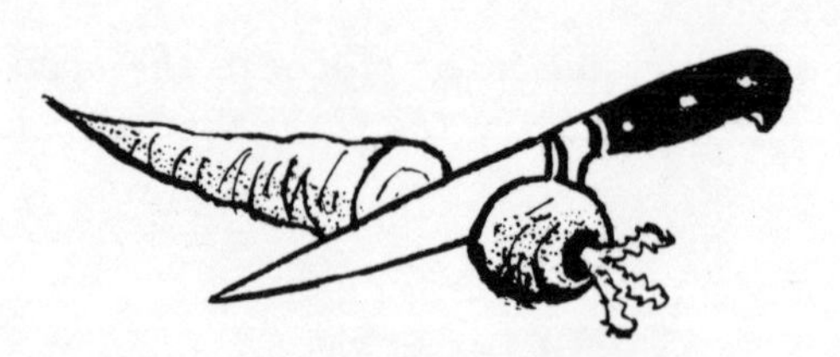

Narcissi

*Put a layer of pebbles in a soup bowl. Then put enough water in the bowl so that the pebbles are nearly covered. Put some narcissi bulbs on top. See exactly what happens: the bulbs send out roots as well as a stem. Record all the developments.*

# St David's Day

St David's Day is 1 March. St David – *Dewi Sant* in Welsh – is the patron saint of Wales. In about A.D. 530 he founded a monastery in a little Pembrokeshire valley called Glyn Rhoslyn, the vale of roses. St David's cathedral church stands near the site of the monastery, in the town of the same name. Many miraculous stories are told about the saint. One legend tells that there was no water near his monastery, but when he prayed, a well appeared by his feet. Ffynnon Feddyg, the doctor's spring, near Aberaeron (Cardiganshire) is said to have burst from the ground at a spot where St David healed the blind, the lame and the sick. He died on 1 March, 589, and his soul, according to legend, was carried to heaven by a host of angels. Ever since, 1 March has been called St David's Day. Many Welshmen wear leeks on this day to commemorate Cadwallader's victory over the Saxons on 1 March. The Britons, under King Cadwallader, at the suggestion of St David, wore leeks to show the side they were on; armies did not wear uniform in those days.

Ruins of the Bishop's Palace, St David's

## Three Jovial Welshmen

Now all that day they hunted and nothing could they find,
Except a ship a-sailing, and that they left behind.

The first he said it was a ship, the second he said "nay",
The third he said it was a house with the chimney all blown away.

Then all the night they hunted and nothing could they find,
Except the moon a-gliding, and that they left behind.

The first he said it was the moon, the second he said "nay",
The third he said it was a cheese with half of it cut away.

Then all next day they hunted and nothing could they find,
But a hedgehog in a bramble bush, and that they left behind.

The first he said it was a hedgehog, the second he said "nay",
The third he said it was a pin-cushion with the pins stuck in the wrong way.

Then all that night they hunted and nothing could they find,
Except an owl in a holly tree, and that they left behind.

The first he said it was an owl, the second he said "nay",
The third he said it was an old man with his beard all growing grey.

from *Children's Songs of Long Ago* by Alfred Moffat and Frank Kidson

*It would be interesting to draw the three men in the song, and the things they saw (or didn't see). Perhaps you could make up some more verses.*

## *Leeks*

Eat leeks in Lide
And ramains in May,
And all the year after
Physicians may play.
Devon Rhyme

(*Lide* = March; *ramains* = wild garlic)

*Do you know, or can you find out, any more rhymes like this about things that are good to eat at certain times of the year?*

*Leeks grow well all over Wales and to this day the leek is a very popular Welsh vegetable. Here is a traditional recipe that you might be able to try out at home on St David's Day:*

Pasteiod Cennin (Leek Pasties)

*12 large leeks (the white part only)*
*1 teaspoon lemon juice*
*1 teaspoon sugar*
*a pinch of sdlt*
*a little cream (optional)*
*1 egg yolk*

For the pastry:
*500 g (4 cups) flour*
*250 g (1 cup) lard, butter, or margarine*
*1 teaspoon baking powder (unless using self-raising flour)*
*a pinch of salt*
*$\frac{1}{8}$ l ($\frac{1}{2}$ cup) cold water*

*Clean the leeks well by holding them under running water and trim them. After trimming the green ends make a cross on that part. Stand them in a deep jug of cold water, green end down, and leave for several hours. Cut the white part into 2·5 cm pieces and cook them in boiling salted water to which the sugar and lemon juice have been added, for not more than five minutes. Then drain well and let them cool.*

*Make the pastry by rubbing the fat into the flour and salt, then add the water slowly, mixing well all the time. Turn out onto a floured board and roll out to a thickness of about 1 cm, then cut into oblongs about 15 cm long and 10 cm wide; this amount should make about twelve. Allow one large leek for each pasty, laying several pieces along the middle of the pastry. If using cream add a very little to each pasty just to moisten it, sprinkle with salt, then wet the edges with water and draw up the sides, pressing well to keep the edges together. Brush over with beaten egg yolk and bake for 15–20 minutes in a hot oven (200°C).*

*This will serve about six.*

*You can add a little chopped bacon to each pasty as well although the pure leek recipe is the real Welsh one.*

adapted from *A Taste of Wales* by Theodora Fitzgibbon

# St Patrick's Day

St Patrick's Day is 17 March. St Patrick is the patron saint of Ireland. He was in fact Scottish by birth, but was captured and sold as a slave in Ireland. Though he left Ireland at the age of twenty-two, he returned when he was fifty-nine, landing at Wicklow in A.D. 432, intending to preach the gospel and convert the Irish to Christianity. He died in about the year 464.

St Patrick is supposed to have rid Ireland of snakes. The last snake resisted him and St Patrick overcame him by a clever trick. He made a small box and asked the snake to get into it. The snake refused, saying it was too small. St Patrick argued that it was not too small and in the end the snake agreed to prove his point by trying to get into the box. Once he was inside, St Patrick snapped the lid shut and threw the box into the sea.

St Patrick's cross is X-shaped, with a red cross on a white background:

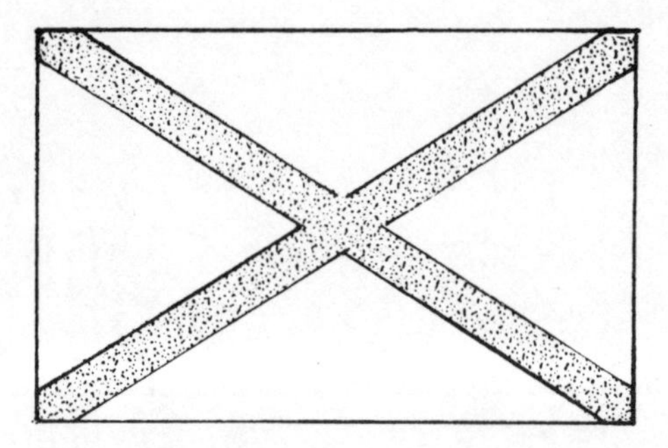

*See if you can find any stories about the patron saints of other countries. When did they live, what things did they do, and what do their flags look like? You could make up a booklet about patron saints with drawings about important things in their lives.*

*The flag of the British Isles, the Union Jack, is made up of the crosses of three of the patron saints. Which were they and how were their crosses put together to form the flag? See what you can find out about its history.*

*As well as the patron saints of countries, many areas of the British Isles have particular saints associated with them. See if there are any in the area where you live and find out what days and stories are especially associated with them. You could make up a booklet about them as well.*

*Make up and act a play dealing with an incident in the life of a patron saint.*

*(See also St George's Day, on pages 36–7.)*

# The Coming of Spring

## Spring Surprises Baron Munchhausen

I remember one snowy winter coming to a part of the country I did not recognize in the darkness and the snow. I dismounted, tied my horse to what looked like a small tree stump and, wrapping my great-coat around me, I lay down and slept.

I did not wake until the morning. Imagine my surprise when I opened my eyes to find myself in a pretty churchyard. How had I come here? And where was my horse? A lonely neigh somewhere above me made me look up, and there he was, tied by the bridle to the church weathercock.

I soon realized what had happened. Spring had come overnight and the snow, which had completely covered the church, had melted away. I had sunk down with the melting snow but my poor horse, tied to what I had believed to be a tree stump, was now dangling by his bridle from the top of the steeple.

Immediately, I took one of my pistols and shot clean through the horse's bridle. He came clattering down the roof and landed on the springy turf, where I mounted him and we trotted on.

## *Make a Mime Play (The Coming of Spring)*

*Imagine you're a snowman, standing in a park. The sun comes out. Slowly you melt.*

*Curl up very small, so that you are as small as a seed in the dark soil. It's very cold. Gradually you feel the sun's warmth. As the sun continues to shine, you begin to open to it. Grow up – unfold – reach for the sun. Feel the sun warming your petals.*

*Imagine you're a squirrel, curled up asleep, snug against the winter. The sun wakes you. Stretch out – accept the sun.*

*The frost comes in winter. Walk about like frost, very sharp and spiky. Gradually feel yourself warming up in the spring air, and make your movements looser and looser.*

*With a partner, act the battle between frost and thaw. Frost is stiff and cold, thaw is loose and warm. Fight in mime – don't actually touch your partner. Thaw wins. Change parts and try it again.*

*In a group, build a snowman. One person is the snowman, he lies very small on the floor. The rest build him up. Build in mime – don't touch the snowman. When you've built him, run away and leave him standing in the cold morning. Then come back as thaw, and melt him. Do it gradually, without actually touching him.*

*When you have done all these different mimes about spring, you can put them together to make a good mime play.*

*Groups: seeds buried in the earth; animals asleep; frost dancing; one or two snowmen standing stiff; thaw.*

*The thaw defeats the frost. It melts the snowman. The seeds grow. The animals awake.*

*This drama will need some practice to be good. You may find a record of suitable music helps, too. Stravinsky's* The Rite of Spring *is a good one to help the mime.*

## Persephone and the Coming of Spring

Demeter is the earth mother. From her comes all life. She is the goddess of all things that grow, and without growth there is no life. The earth mother generates life in the dead seed, pushes up the corn stalks, turns them to gold for the harvester to take and make into bread. All life comes from the good will of the earth mother.

Demeter had one daughter, Persephone, whose hair was golden as the corn, and who was so beautiful that men called her the Flower Maiden. They lived together in a world full of light and dancing flowers.

Under the earth in a gloomy cave palace lived Hades, god of the underworld. His kingdom was hell. It was always twilight there and Hades envied the golden earth mother and her beautiful flower maiden daughter. Besides, Hades wanted a wife.

One day, when Persephone had wandered off alone to pick flowers, Hades below the earth saw her. He harnessed horses to his dark chariot and galloped up to the earth. Persephone heard the hoofbeats thudding on the earth and looked round. The great chariot was over her like a black landslide. She screamed, but he was upon her. He leaned out from the speeding chariot, gathered the defenceless girl in his arm and swung her easily into his chariot.

She screamed for help, screamed and screamed, and Hades urged on his horses with his cutting whip. They galloped in a frenzy towards the gates of hell, lashed by the whip, frightened by the screams. As they disappeared down the dark shaft to the kingdom under the earth, Demeter, the earth mother, heard her daughter's cry.

She looked up, stared, but saw nothing, for Persephone had gone with Hades. She only heard, echoing through and through her head, that last despairing cry which her daughter had cried when she left the bright world behind her. Then Demeter flew into a rage. She walked the earth, north and south, west and east, searching for her daughter, madly seeking everywhere, and the bright things growing on the earth seemed to mock her search. She could not find Persephone, so, in her great anger, she cursed the flowers, the trees, the crops, even the grass. And when Demeter, the earth mother, cursed the living things which grew, they shrivelled and withered and died.

No more flowers, only bent brown petals which crumbled if an insect landed on them. No more leafy trees, only jagged spiky skeletons without fruit, without nests. No more golden corn for the harvester, no grass for the cattle. The earth died. The ploughman broke the clods in vain. The cattle, tugging the brown grass, got no nourishment. The earth died.

And then men and animals began to die, too. Demeter watched with cold fury. She cared nothing for men or animals. She wanted her daughter. She let men die.

In the underworld, Hades had his prize, Persephone, but she gave nothing to him. She refused to sleep with him, she refused to eat with him. She wandered through the cold twilight of Hades' kingdom alone, wasting away. One day, she saw a ripe pomegranate, and picked it. It reminded her of the fruit of the earth. Peeling away the rind, she ate seven seeds. But they tasted bitter to her, and she threw the rest away.

Zeus, king of the gods, saw his earth changing to a charnel-house. He knew why Demeter, earth mother, gave no more life, and he went to see Hades, his brother, in the underworld. He told Hades how the earth was dying, how he would have no men to rule over, nor would Hades have any more dead souls come to his kingdom, if Persephone was not returned.

But Hades replied that she could not return. He wanted her. Besides, she had eaten here in his kingdom under the earth – and once a person has eaten in the kingdom under the earth, that person may never return to the light.

"I've never touched the food you gave me," said Persephone.

"No," agreed Hades, "but you ate seven seeds of the pomegranate."

What could Zeus do? The earth must blossom and bear fruit again, or all life would die. But because Persephone had eaten in the kingdom of the dead, she could not return to earth, and without Persephone, the earth mother had sworn to remain sterile. In the end Zeus found a solution. He led Persephone up through the profound tunnels of hell and out into the bright air. When her mother saw her, she was overcome with joy, she embraced her, and brought growth to the plants, sap to the trees. So the world blossomed again, and in half a year the harvest was brought in, the world was full of light and dancing flowers again.

But at the end of the half year, Persephone had to return to Hades, and the earth mother cursed the world again. The ground yielded nothing. The earth died. Winter came. But it lasted only half a year, for then Persephone returned to her mother and spring came again.

And every year since then, Persephone has returned for half the year. When she returns, the earth mother generates life in the dead seed, pushes up the corn stalks, turns them to gold for the harvester to take and make into bread, and all life begins again, for it is spring.

## *Thinking, Talking, Writing about Spring*

*What are the first signs of spring?*

*Make notes about early flowers. Which flowers are the first to appear? Draw them, or describe them in writing.*

*Choose one or two particular flowers which you see every day. Record what happens to them each day. For instance, you might measure how tall they are at the same time each day; you could photograph or draw them every two or three days, and write a description of them each day as they grow.*

*Try recording the progress of a bird's nest as it is being built – but be careful not to alarm the bird, or it won't go on building there.*

### The Missel-thrush's Nest

In early March, before the lark
Dare start, beside the huge oak tree,
Close fixed agen the powdered bark,
The mavis' nest I often see;
And mark, as wont, the bits of wool
Hang round about its early bed;
She lays six eggs in colours dull,
Blotched thick with spots of burning red.

from *The Shepherd's Calendar* by John Clare

*Do people behave differently when spring comes? Try to notice whether people dress differently, and if they do, in what ways.*

*What games do children play in spring?*

*Imagine what a small child might think about the coming of spring. What might an elderly person think?*

*How would you describe what happens in spring to a blind person? How could a blind person use his other senses to help him?*

*What would you write in a description of spring for a deaf person?*

## *Frog-spawn*

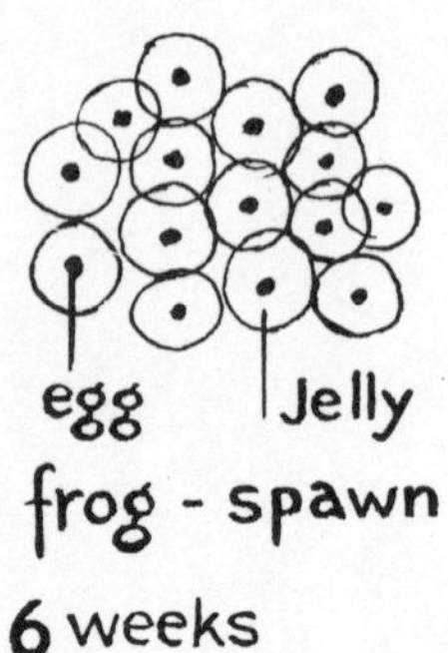


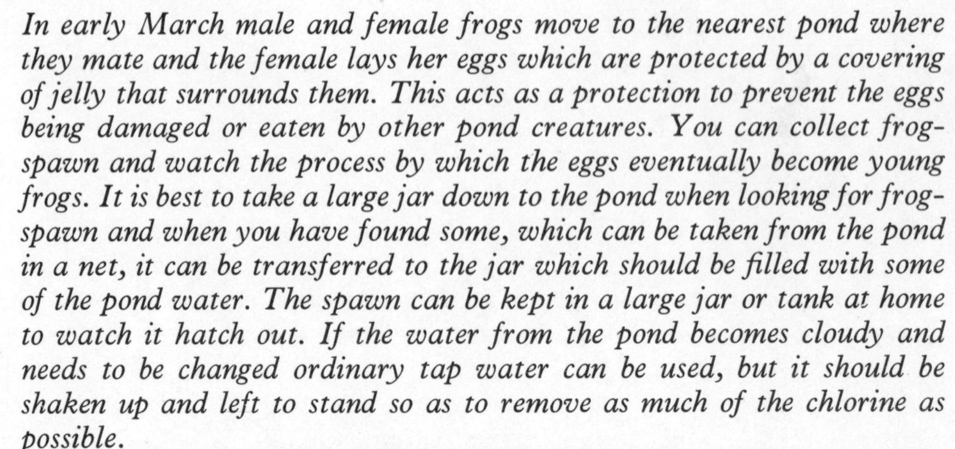

*In early March male and female frogs move to the nearest pond where they mate and the female lays her eggs which are protected by a covering of jelly that surrounds them. This acts as a protection to prevent the eggs being damaged or eaten by other pond creatures. You can collect frog-spawn and watch the process by which the eggs eventually become young frogs. It is best to take a large jar down to the pond when looking for frog-spawn and when you have found some, which can be taken from the pond in a net, it can be transferred to the jar which should be filled with some of the pond water. The spawn can be kept in a large jar or tank at home to watch it hatch out. If the water from the pond becomes cloudy and needs to be changed ordinary tap water can be used, but it should be shaken up and left to stand so as to remove as much of the chlorine as possible.*

*After about ten days the jelly will become more liquid and the tadpoles can be seen moving about inside. They will gradually emerge completely and the jar or tank should have some pond weed put inside it for the tadpoles to feed on. It is also advisable to put in some raw meat as the tadpoles are flesh-eaters and will eat each other if nothing else is provided for them. At this stage the water should be changed every few days or whenever it begins to get cloudy.*

*About two months after hatching, the tadpoles will frequently come to the surface to gulp air into their newly formed lungs. At this time it is important to put some sticks poking out of the tank into the water so that the young frog, which will appear in about a month's time, can climb out onto the land. At this stage it ought to be put in some damp and long grass near a pond so that it can begin to grow into an adult frog; it will be about four years before it is an adult old enough to breed and start the process all over again. The change of the tadpole into a frog is a process known as* metamorphosis. *The accompanying diagrams show the stages that are involved as the change takes place and you should see how far your tadpoles fit this timescale.*

6 weeks

8 weeks

10·11 weeks

12 weeks

## Spring

Spring, the sweet Spring, is the year's pleasant king;
Then blooms each thing; then maids dance in a ring,
Cold doth not sting, the pretty birds do sing:
  Cuckoo, jug-jug, pu-we, to-witta-woo!

The palm and may make country houses gay,
Lambs frisk and play, the shepherds pipe all day,
And we hear aye birds tune this merry lay:
  Cuckoo, jug-jug, pu-we, to-witta-woo!

The fields breathe sweet, the daisies kiss our feet,
Young lovers meet, old wives a-sunning sit;
In every street these tunes our ears do greet:
  Cuckoo, jug-jug, pu-we, to-witta-woo!
    Spring, the sweet Spring!

Thomas Nashe

# Mothering Sunday

Mothering Sunday is the fourth Sunday in Lent and ought not to be confused with the more modern Mother's Day, which was invented in America in 1906, and which has become a very commercial occasion when children are urged to buy presents for their mothers. Flowers, in particular, tend to be sold at very expensive prices. Since then, all kinds of other similar days have been invented, such as Father's Day, and each of them is accompanied by cards in the same way as Christmas or St Valentine's Day.

But the proper Mothering Sunday is a very old festival that goes back to pre-Christian times when a festival was held to celebrate "the Mother of the Gods". In Christian times this became a day especially dedicated to Mother Church when the church would be decorated with flowers, something to cheer us up in the gloom of Lent.

Later still, it became a day when servants and apprentices were given a day off to go to visit their mothers. They took with them gifts, usually small bunches of flowers, often wild flowers gathered from the hedgerows, and a *simnel cake*.

## *How to Make a Simnel Cake*

*150 g flour*
*100 g butter*
*100 g sugar*
*3 eggs*
*100 g sultanas*
*50 g currants*
*100 g seedless raisins*
*50 g chopped mixed peel*
*½ teaspoon mixed spice*
*1 tablespoon brandy or rum*
*pinch salt*
*1 level teaspoon baking powder*
*almond paste*
*royal icing*

*Cream sugar and butter, add 2 beaten eggs and flour sifted with the salt and baking powder. Stir in all the other ingredients except the remaining egg, almond paste and icing. If the mixture is too stiff, add a little milk. Line an 18 cm cake tin with greaseproof paper and put in half the cake mixture. Cover with a layer of about a third of the almond paste and put the rest of the cake mixture on top. Bake in a moderate oven for 30 minutes, then reduce oven to slow and bake for a further 2 hours. Take out the cake and leave on a wire cake-cooler. When quite cold, cover the top with the remaining almond paste, decorating the edge with egg-shaped pieces of almond paste. Brush all over with a beaten egg diluted with a little water and put into a hot oven for a few minutes to brown the top. When cool, pour the icing on to the centre of the cake and then decorate with yellow chicks, tiny nests of Easter eggs, angelica and anything else suitable.*

The more traditional decoration for the cake, however, is twelve balls of marzipan which are said to represent the twelve Apostles; sometimes they are reduced to eleven to exclude Judas. But we know that similar cakes were being made at least as far back as Roman times.

Certainly they were well known in the time of the poet, Herrick, who mentions them (and the custom of mothering) in one of his poems:

> I'le to thee a Simnell bring,
> 'Gainst thou go'st a mothering.
> So that, when she blesseth thee,
> Half that blessing thou'lt give me.

# Carling Sunday

The fifth Sunday in Lent is known as Carling Sunday which is another way of saying "care" Sunday. The word "care" here means trouble or suffering and it was a day on which the suffering of Jesus was especially remembered. But it was also the day, especially in the north of England, on which people ate dried peas fried in butter which were known as "carlings".

James Kirkup recalls his childhood:

At South Shields, on the Friday before Carling Sunday all the little grocer's shops would have a big dish of carls or carlings for sale: they were small, brownish-yellow wrinkled peas which I believe were soaked in sea-water; some people fried them in margarine. They were always sold wet, and if you wanted to buy some it was best to take a bowl or jug to carry them home in. They were sold at a penny a pint, and were very popular with "the kids", who used them as ammunition for their pea-shooters. Carling Sunday always marked the opening of the pea-shooting season, just as April Fool's Day heralded the beginning of the "hoop and guard" days, Whit Monday the top-and-whip, and 5th November the Jack-o'-Lantern.

I never liked carlings. I don't think any of us did, really, though children often like to eat odd and unpleasant things simply because they are told not to. . . . They were hard and insipid and were said to give you the "dye yer 'air" – diarrhoea. Nevertheless, children ate them in large quantities; it was a ritual, a tradition, and traditions are things which children do not willingly abandon.

from *The Only Child* by James Kirkup

*Are there particular foods that you traditionally eat on certain days? What are they?*

## *Peashooters*

*Nowadays you can buy metal peashooters in the shops but it is better to make them for yourself. They can easily be made out of bamboo cane like this:*

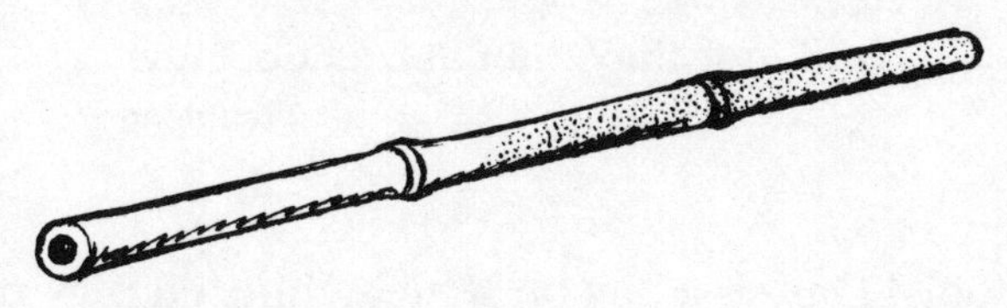

*Or the hollow stem of a plant like "kexy" can be used instead. "Kexy" is an old name for the dry, hollow stem of certain plants such as cow parsley.*

WARNING: Be careful only to use cow parsley for this purpose, as some hollow-stemmed plants are poisonous.

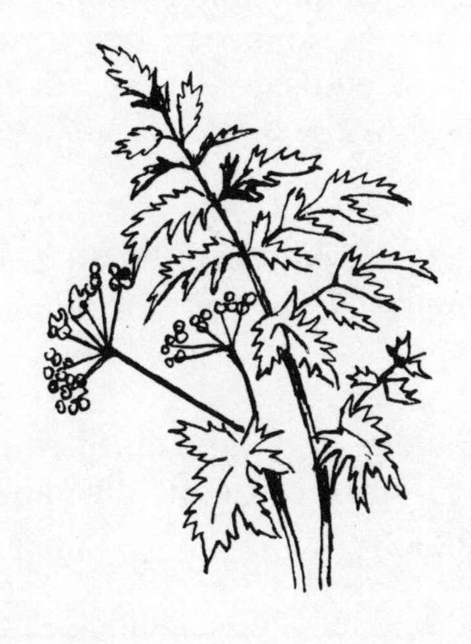

## The Saddest Noise, The Sweetest Noise

The saddest noise, the sweetest noise,
The maddest noise that grows,
The birds, they make it in the Spring,
At night's delicious close

Between the March and April line,
The magical frontier
Beyond which summer hesitates,
Almost too heavenly near.

Emily Dickinson

# All Fools' Day

The first April, some do say,
Is set apart for All Fools' Day;
But why the people call it so,
Nor I, nor they themselves do know.

Traditional

1 April, All Fools' Day, is a day on which children play tricks on each other and on grown-ups, as this fourteen-year-old boy describes:

It is a day when you hoax friends of yours with jokes like sending them to the shop for some pigeon's milk, or telling them to dig a hole because the dog has died; when they come back and ask where is the dead dog you say "April fool" and laugh at them. There are some when you just say "Your shoe lace is undone" or "Your belt is hanging" or "Go and fetch that plate off the table", and of course their shoe lace is tied up right, and their belt is not hanging, and there is no plate on the table, so you say "Ever been had, April fool."

from *The Lore and Language of Schoolchildren* by I. and P. Opie

*What tricks have you played on April Fool's Day? Make a list of as many typical April Fool's tricks as you can think of.*

The period of April foolery only lasts until midday, twelve o'clock. After that, if you try to make someone else an April Fool you may hear this rhyme in reply:

April Fool's gone and past
You're the biggest fool at last;
When April Fool's Day comes again,
You'll be the biggest fool then.

*Are there any similar rhymes in your part of the country? See if you can make a collection of any of them known to members of the class.*

*Find a copy of Bruegel's painting* Children's Games. *As a group, try to make a drawing showing children playing April Fools' jokes on each other in the same way. How many games in the picture can you recognize and how many of them do you play today?*

## April the First

Fool's Day, and here – the opening chorus;
Mouths wide open; the only silent parts
Are for the dead and they, at bright moments,
Come half-way back; every fence and stile
Seems able to air new leaves. For a while the old
Wizard repeats his annual round of tricks –
Pulls legs, lambs, chicks out of a hat –
And laughs until the tears run down his cheeks.
"How does he do it? how does he pull it off?"
We murmur; "every year the same patter,
The identical apparitions – but not stale;
Like a refrain, rather than a time-worn tale,
Its touch grows headier with each repetition."
And the magic? – that is real, not fake: search him,
You'll find no chicks or rabbits up his sleeve, –
In fact, you'll find no sleeve; no wizard, even;
Only the magic that from an empty hat
Tips tons of blossom, and the dawn chorus,
And open mouths that threaten to eat up
The struggling harvest and come back for more.
No wonder some will not believe their eyes;
Or make believe they're not impressed, and say
"Let's stuff that rubbish back into the hat."

Edward Lowbury

# Mr Vinegar

Mr and Mrs Vinegar lived in a vinegar bottle. Now, one day, when Mr Vinegar was from home, Mrs Vinegar, who was a very good housewife, was busily sweeping her house, when an unlucky thump of the broom brought the whole house clitter-clatter, clitter-clatter, about her ears. In an agony of grief she rushed forth to meet her husband. On seeing him she exclaimed, "Oh, Mr Vinegar, Mr Vinegar, we are ruined, we are ruined: I have knocked the house down, and it is all to pieces!" Mr Vinegar then said: "My dear, let us see what can be done. Here is the door. I will take it on my back, and we will go forth to seek our fortune." They walked all that day, and at nightfall entered a thick forest. They were both very, very tired, and Mr Vinegar said: "My love, I will climb up into a tree, drag up the door, and you shall follow." He accordingly did so, and they both stretched their weary limbs on the door, and fell fast asleep. In the middle of the night Mr Vinegar was disturbed by the sound of voices underneath, and to his horror and dismay found that it was a band of thieves met to divide their booty. "Here, Jack," said one, "here's five pounds for you. Here, Bill, here's ten pounds for you. Here, Bob, here's three pounds for you." Mr Vinegar could listen no longer. His terror was so great that he trembled and trembled, and shook down the door on their heads. Away scampered the thieves, but Mr Vinegar dared not quit his retreat till broad daylight. He then scrambled out of the tree, and went to lift up the door. What did he see but a number of golden guineas. "Come down, Mrs Vinegar," he cried, "come down, I say. Our fortune's made, our fortune's made! Come down, I say." Mrs Vinegar got down as fast as she could, and when she saw the money she jumped for joy. "Now, my dear," said she, "I'll tell you what you shall do. There is a fair at the neighbouring town. You shall take these forty guineas and buy a cow. I can make butter and cheese, which you shall sell at market, and we shall then be able to live very comfortably." Mr Vinegar joyfully agreed, took the money, and off he went to the fair. When he arrived, he walked up and down, and at length saw a beautiful red cow. It was an excellent milker, and perfect in every way. "Oh," thought Mr Vinegar, "if I had but that cow, I should be the happiest man alive." So he offers the forty guineas for the cow, and the owner said that, as he was a friend, he'd oblige him. So the bargain was made, and he got the cow and he drove it backwards and forwards to show it. By-and-by he saw a man playing the bagpipes – Tweedle-dum tweedle-dee. The children followed him about, and he appeared to be pocketing money on all sides. "Well," thought Mr Vinegar, "if I had but that beautiful instrument I should be the happiest man alive – my fortune would be made." So he went up to the man. "Friend," says he, "what a beautiful instrument that is, and what a deal of money you must make." "Why, yes," said the man, "I make a great deal of money, to be sure, and it is a wonderful instrument." "Oh!" cried Mr Vinegar, "how I should like to possess it!" "Well," said the man, "as you are a friend, I don't much mind parting with it. You shall have it for that red cow." "Done!" said the delighted Mr Vinegar. So the beautiful red cow was given for the bagpipes. He walked up and down with his purchase but it was in vain he tried to play a tune, and instead of pocketing pence, the boys followed him hooting, laughing, and pelting.

Poor Mr Vinegar, his fingers grew very cold, and, just as he was leaving the town, he met a man with a fine thick pair of gloves. "Oh, my fingers are so very cold," said Mr Vinegar to himself. "Now if I had but those beautiful gloves I should be the happiest man alive." He went up to the man, and said to him: "Friend, you seem to have a capital pair of gloves there." "Yes, truly," cried the man, "and my hands are as warm as possible this cold March day." "Well," said Mr Vinegar, "I should like to have them." "What will you give?" said the man. "As you are a friend, I don't much mind letting you have them for those bagpipes." "Done!" cried Mr Vinegar. He put on the gloves, and felt perfectly happy as he trudged homewards.

At last he grew very tired, when he saw a man coming towards him with a good stout stick in his hand.

"Oh," said Mr Vinegar, "that I had but that stick! I should then be the happiest man alive." He said to the man: "Friend! what a rare good stick you have got." "Yes," said the man, "I have used it for many a long mile, and a good friend it has been, but if you have a fancy for it, as you are a friend, I don't mind giving it to you for that pair of gloves." Mr Vinegar's hands were so warm, and his legs so tired, that he gladly made the exchange. As he drew near to the wood where he had left his wife, he heard a parrot on a tree calling out his name: "Mr Vinegar, you foolish man, you blockhead, you simpleton, you went to the fair, and laid out all your money in buying a cow. Not content with that, you changed it for bagpipes, on which you could not play, and which were not worth one-tenth of the money. You fool, you – you had no sooner got the bagpipes than you changed them for the gloves, which were not worth one-quarter of the money, and when you had got the gloves, you changed them for a poor miserable stick, and now for your forty guineas, cow, bagpipes, and gloves, you have nothing to show but that poor miserable stick, which you might have cut in any hedge." On this the bird laughed and laughed, and Mr Vinegar, falling into a violent rage, threw the stick at its head. The stick lodged in the tree, and he returned to his wife without money, cow, bagpipes, gloves, or stick, and she instantly gave him such a sound cudgelling that she almost broke every bone in his skin.

from *English Fairy Tales*, collected by Joseph Jacobs

# Maundy Thursday

Maundy Thursday is the Thursday before Good Friday. It is well-known for the "Royal Maundy" which usually takes place at Westminster Abbey. Originally the king or queen went to the Abbey to wash the feet of the poor in memory of Christ washing his disciples' feet. However, since 1689, that ceremony has been replaced by giving away specially minted money, known as Maundy Money. The people to receive the money are chosen from London parishes and are presented with silver penny, twopenny, threepenny and fourpenny coins to a total value of one penny for each year of the sovereign's age. The coins are legal tender but are hardly ever spent and complete sets of them are greatly valued by collectors.

In the ceremony a Yeoman of the Guard carries a golden tray containing a number of leather purses, some of which are white and some red. The Maundy Money is in the white purses and in the others there is some ordinary money given instead of the food and clothing that used to be handed out to the poor. Those taking part in the ceremony carry a posy of flowers and herbs to protect them against the plague and the clergymen carry linen towels on their shoulders as a reminder of the origin of the ceremony.

The Queen at the Royal Maundy Ceremony

## Holy Thursday

'Twas on a Holy Thursday, their innocent faces clean,
The children walking two and two, in red and blue and green,
Grey-headed beadles walk'd before, with wands as white as snow,
Till into the high dome of Paul's they like Thames' waters flow.

O what a multitude they seem'd, these flowers of London town!
Seated in companies they sit with radiance all their own.
The hum of multitudes was there, but multitudes of lambs,
Thousands of little boys and girls raising their innocent hands.

Now like a mighty wind they raise to Heaven the voice of song,
Or like harmonious thunderings the seats of Heaven among.
Beneath them sit the aged men, wise guardians of the poor;
Then cherish pity, lest you drive an angel from your door.

William Blake

# Good Friday

This is the Friday before Easter Sunday and is the day on which the Church especially remembers the Crucifixion of Christ. The word "Good" here really means "Holy" Friday and there is an old superstition that those born on this day have the power of seeing and commanding spirits.

Hot Cross Buns are eaten on Good Friday to remind us of the Cross of Christ. They were said to keep a whole year without going mouldy and some people hung one or more of them in their house to keep evil spirits away:

> Good Friday comes this month: the old woman runs
> With one a penny, two a penny "hot cross buns".
> Whose virtue is, if you believe what's said,
> They'll not grow mouldy like the common bread.
>
> from *Poor Robin's Almanack*, 1733

Here is a nineteenth-century recipe for Hot Cross Buns which you might like to try although we will not guarantee that they will keep for a year! Equivalent metric quantities for the ingredients have been added.

*1 lb (500g) flour*
*a pinch of salt*
*1 level teaspoon powdered cinnamon*
*1 level teaspoon mixed spice*
*2 oz (25g) butter*
*2 oz (25g) currants*
*2 oz (25g) yeast*
*2 tablespoons caster sugar*
*about ½ pint (250 ml) milk*
*1 egg*

*Sieve the flour with salt and spices, rub in the butter and add the currants. Cream the yeast with a little of the sugar, add a little warm milk and pour in the centre of the flour, sprinkle lightly over with flour and leave for 10 minutes. Then mix to a stiff dough with the beaten egg, adding a little milk if required.*

*Allow to rise until the mixture doubles itself in size. Divide into portions, mould into small buns, mark with a cross, cutting fairly deeply, and place on a greased and floured tin. Allow to rise until half as large again. Bake in a hot oven, 220°C, gas mark 7, for 5 to 8 minutes. Melt a little sugar in 1 tablespoon of milk and brush over the buns.*

## The Widow's Son Tavern

In about 1800 there was a widow who lived in a little cottage on Devons Road, Bromley-by-Bow, London. She had one son, who was a sailor. When Easter time drew near, she made her hot cross buns, and as she was expecting her son home, she put one aside for him. But he did not return, though no one could say for certain that he was dead. So the widow continued to hope.

A year went by, and still the son did not come home. When she made her hot cross buns, she again set one aside for him, and hung it from the beam on the ceiling where she had kept the other. But he did not come home that year, or the next, or the next after that, and each year the widow made him another bun and hung it with the rest.

He never did come back, and when the widow died, the other people living in Bun House as it was now called kept up the tradition. When the cottage was knocked down, a public house was built on the site, and it was called The Widow's Son. The buns were saved and hung up in the pub, where the custom has continued ever since. Every Good Friday a sailor is asked to add a hot cross bun to the collection, which is now very large, particularly as others have been added on special occasions, such as the Relief of Mafeking and the coronation of Queen Elizabeth II.

## Some Good Friday Superstitions

Good Friday is a specially good day for planting crops, particularly potatoes, because Satan has no power over the earth on this day. But if a housewife washes clothes on Good Friday, she may find them spotted with Christ's blood.

Friday is the unluckiest day of the week, because Christ was crucified on a Friday. Friday the thirteenth is especially unlucky because there were thirteen people at the last supper.

# Easter

Easter is what is known as a "moveable feast". Its date changes each year depending upon when the Church celebrates Easter and this of course affects all the other dates that depend upon the date of Easter, such as Ash Wednesday, Good Friday and Whitsun. It is also the reason why the spring term in schools is sometimes very short and sometimes very long. Easter Sunday, in fact, is the first day after the full moon which happens upon or next after 21 March. If the full moon occurs on a Sunday, Easter Day is the Sunday after. It will always fall between 22 March and 25 April.

*Many people think that it would make things easier if we could agree to celebrate Easter on the same date every year – "a fixed Easter". What are your views on whether we should have a fixed Easter or not?*

*The Book of Common Prayer gives instructions for finding the date on which Easter will occur but you might find the following table an easier way of looking it up. The table also gives dates for other "moveable feasts":*

| | Shrove Tuesday | Mothering Sunday | Palm Sunday | Easter Day | Whitsun |
|---|---|---|---|---|---|
| **1978** | 7 Feb | 6 Mar | 19 Mar | 26 Mar | 14 May |
| **1979** | 27 Feb | 25 Mar | 8 Apr | 15 Apr | 3 June |
| **1980** | 18 Feb | 16 Mar | 30 Mar | 6 Apr | 25 May |
| **1981** | 3 Mar | 29 Mar | 12 Apr | 19 Apr | 7 June |
| **1982** | 23 Feb | 21 Mar | 4 Apr | 11 Apr | 30 May |
| **1983** | 15 Feb | 13 Mar | 27 Mar | 3 Apr | 22 May |
| **1984** | 6 Mar | 1 Apr | 15 Apr | 22 Apr | 10 June |
| **1985** | 19 Feb | 17 Mar | 30 Mar | 7 Apr | 26 May |
| **1986** | 11 Feb | 9 Mar | 23 Mar | 30 Mar | 18 May |
| **1987** | 3 Mar | 29 Mar | 12 Apr | 19 Apr | 7 June |
| **1988** | 15 Feb | 13 Mar | 27 Mar | 3 Apr | 22 May |
| **1989** | 7 Feb | 5 Mar | 19 Mar | 26 Mar | 14 May |
| **1990** | 27 Feb | 25 Mar | 8 Apr | 15 Apr | 3 June |

## Easter Eggs

Although Easter is one of the most important dates in the Christian calendar when the resurrection of Christ is remembered, the festival itself is much older than this. It was originally a celebration of the coming of spring. The Anglo-Saxons called it Eosturmonath, a feast in celebration of the goddess of spring, Eostre. Similar festivals to celebrate the coming of spring have been held throughout the world and go back to very ancient times.

Because eggs are connected with the coming of new life it is natural that they should be associated with this season and this tradition also goes back far beyond Christian times. But eggs were forbidden as food during the fast period of Lent and this is why they were especially given as presents when the coming of Easter marked the end of Lent. Today decorated and chocolate eggs are usually given instead.

### *Decorated Eggs*

*Long before the modern chocolate egg had been invented people gave each other "pace eggs", the word "pace" coming from "paschal" which is another name for Easter. These were hard-boiled eggs with a decorated shell, or they were boiled in such a way as to dye the shells. You can easily make some pace eggs for yourself by boiling eggs in water containing different things to provide the dye. For example, if you boil eggs in water containing onion skins they will end up a mottled brown on the outside. If you use gorse flowers, they will be bright yellow, and if you use cochineal they will come out deep crimson. A dish of various coloured eggs on the breakfast table is a cheerful start to Easter morning.*

*It is even easier to colour the outside shell of hard-boiled eggs with felt markers so as to decorate them with patterns or faces.*

### *A Chocolate Hen's Egg*

*A more unusual idea is to produce an egg that looks like an ordinary hen's egg on the outside but turns out to have a chocolate egg inside. You can make one of these by carefully piercing both ends of the egg with a darning needle and very gently blowing out the contents into a basin. Then rinse the eggshell gently and allow it to dry out. Block up one hole with a piece of tape. After this, gently pour melted chocolate into the egg through a small funnel – it is easiest to do this if the egg is standing in an eggcup. When the chocolate has set you will have a chocolate egg inside an eggshell.*

*How many other ways can you think of or discover to decorate eggs?*

## Pace Egging

All kinds of fun can be had with the hard-boiled decorated pace eggs, apart from eating them. In some parts of the country it was the custom for children to go round begging for Easter eggs, or their equivalent in goods or money:

### Pace Egg Song

Come search up your money,
Be jubilant and free,
And give us your pace egg
For Easter Monday.

Go down in your cellars
And see what you'll find,
If your barrels be empty
I hope you'll provide;
I hope you'll provide
Sweet eggs and strong beer
And we'll come no more to you
Until the next year.

These times they are hard
And money is scant,
But one pace egg of yours
Is all that we want;

And if you will grant us
This little small thing,
We'll all charm our voices
And merry we'll sing.

Just look at St George
So brisk and so bold,
While in his right hand
A sword he doth hold;
A star on his breast
Like silver doth shine,
And I hope you'll remember
It's pace egging time.

Come search up your money
And see that it's right:
If you give nowt we'll tak nowt:
Farewell and goodnight.

collected by Roy Palmer

**First and last verses begin here.*

This song comes from Midgley, near Halifax, West Yorkshire. It is sung by the performers at the end of the Pace Egg Play, which is very like the Christmas mumming play (see the *Winter* volume of *Feasts & Seasons*). Saint George is the hero of the play, which is performed in the streets of the local towns and villages – Midgley, Hebden Bridge, Mytholmroyd, Luddenden – every Good Friday by boys from the Calder High School, Mytholmroyd.

Boys from Calder High School, Mytholmroyd, performing the Pace Egg Play

## Egg Games for Easter

*Other customs that take place in some parts of the country include hiding the eggs in the garden for the children to find or rolling the hard-boiled eggs down a hill to see whose egg remains unbroken the longest. Another thing that sometimes happens is the playing of a game with the eggs known as "jarping", which is rather like conkers. Each person holds a pace egg firmly in his hand and knocks it against his opponent's to see which is the strongest and which egg can score the most victims. In some places the winner takes as his own any eggs he succeeds in breaking in this way.*

*There may be some traditional customs associated with Easter eggs where you live. If not, you might like to try out some of the games just described – or invent some others for yourselves.*

## Heaving

On Easter Mondays and Tuesdays there was a custom called "heaving" or "lifting". A writer was scandalized by this in 1784:

*Lifting* was originally designed to represent our Saviour's resurrection. The men lift the women on Easter Monday, and the women the men on Tuesday. One or more take hold of each leg, and one or more of each arm, near the body, and lift the person up into a horizontal position *three* times. It is a rude, indecent, and dangerous diversion, practised chiefly by the lower class of people. Our magistrates constantly prohibit it by the bellman, but it subsists at the end of the town.

from *Lancashire Legends* by J. Harland and T. T. Wilkinson

*This was in Clitheroe, Lancashire. What do you think a bellman was?*

At Kidderminster, in Worcestershire, a chair was provided:

Easter Monday was called Heaving Day and was the privileged day for the women . . . they decked themselves gaily for the occasion, dressed a chair with ribbons, and placed a rope across the street; any man bold enough to come within yards of them was caught, placed in the chair, which was then lifted up, turned three times, and finally set down; the terms of release were then settled. The custom was observed in the streets of the town till about the middle of the nineteenth century; in the factories the custom was kept up much longer.

from *British Calendar Customs: England* vol. 1 by A. R. Wright and T. E. Lones

*You might like to try playing a "heaving" game for yourselves*

# The Country Code

*As the days get warmer and longer, you will spend more time outside. If you go into the countryside, remember these ten points of the country code which is designed to reduce or prevent unintentional damage to the countryside:*

1. *Guard against all risks of fire.*
2. *Fasten all gates.*
3. *Keep dogs under proper control.*
4. *Keep to the paths across farm land.*
5. *Avoid damaging fences, hedges and walls.*
6. *Leave no litter.*
7. *Safeguard water supplies.*
8. *Protect wild life, wild plants and trees.*
9. *Go carefully on country roads.*
10. *Respect the life of the countryside.*

## *Trees*

Loveliest of trees, the cherry now
Is hung with bloom along the bough,
And stands about the woodland ride
Wearing white for Eastertide.

A. E. Housman

*Blossom is one of the sights especially associated with spring. How many kinds of blossom can be seen in your area? Collect sprigs of blossom to decorate your classroom. Note the date when each kind of blossom comes out and the differences between the various kinds.*

*The trees also show buds at this time of year. Find out what buds are. Choose a particular bud that you can see easily every day and record carefully how it changes from day to day. Does the weather make any difference to its development?*

# Spring Birds

## *The Cuckoo*

*The cuckoo is probably the best known spring bird – you will find other references to him in this book in the poem "Spring" (page 15), in the "Cottesmore May Song" (page 42) and in the extract from "The Shepherd's Calendar" (page 51). Every year people write letters to the papers claiming to have heard the first cuckoo of the year. Note when you first hear its call this year.*

*The cuckoo never builds his own nest, but lays in other birds' nests and lets them rear his young. It is said that if a girl wants to know how many years will pass before she marries, she should count the number of times she hears the cuckoo. What can you find out about the cuckoo?*

Cuckoo chick being fed by meadow pipit

## *The Swallow*

*You can recognize the swallow by its darting flight and its forked tail. It has a black back, white breast and belly, reddish throat and forehead and a blue-black band below its throat. It eats insects, swooping on them in mid-air as it flies. Its nest, which is saucer-shaped, is made of mud, held together with bits of straw and grass and lined with soft feathers. Usually a swallow builds its nest on a convenient ledge in the shelter of a house or other building. It lays four or five long white eggs, flecked with brown. Its song is high-pitched and twittery.*

*Swallows are often confused with swifts and house-martins. What are the differences between these birds? Write an account of the swift and the house-martin, including a description of their markings, and notes about what they eat, their nesting habits, their eggs and their song. Illustrate your writing by drawing an accurate picture.*

*What other birds return to Britain in the spring? You could make a small book about British migratory birds and illustrate it with coloured drawings.*

# St George's Day

St George is the patron Saint of England. He is commemorated on 23 April.

## St George and the Dragon

When the pagan Roman Empire covered the known world, one of its provinces, the land of Egypt, was terrorized by a mighty dragon.

This huge scaly monster lived in a great lake and from time to time it emerged, breathing fire and squirting poison, looking for food.

At first the people tried to content it by offering it sheep and cattle, but after a time all these were devoured. Then the King of Egypt called his people together to give them his decree – each day, two young people would be sacrificed to the dragon's appetite. The victims would be chosen by lot and no young person might escape.

The day came when the lot fell upon the king's own daughter, the beautiful Sabra. The king tried to excuse her, but the people would not let him. He pleaded and bargained, but they remained firm.

So, weeping and in despair, the king dressed his daughter in bridal robes, led her out to the place of the sacrifice, chained her to a rock, and left her.

A short time afterwards, the fair Sabra heard galloping hooves approaching and, looking round, saw a handsome young warrior riding up. He hailed her, and asked her what was the matter. She told him the story of the fearful dragon.

The stranger swore to save her, in spite of her pleas that he should ride away, for he declared that his god, Jesus Christ, could overcome any beast, fabulous or natural.

Soon the waters of the lake churned and bubbled, then parted, as the green scaly monster rose up for his food. He snorted puffs of flame at the brown-burned grass.

The strange warrior made the sign of the cross, set his lance in its rest and charged the beast. His aim was true. The point of the lance, entering the dragon's throat, penetrated deep into its body. Then he drew his sword and wounded it still further.

The beautiful princess Sabra could hardly believe her eyes when he turned to her, untied her and, threading the rope which had bound her to the rock round the dragon's neck, bade her lead it like a lapdog back to the king's palace. He himself walked beside her with his horse.

As they walked he told her that his name was George, that he was a Christian from Cappadocia, and that it was the might of his god which had enabled him to overcome the dragon.

When they reached the city where the king's palace was, the people, seeing the dragon, prepared to flee. But George called them to stop, declaring that the dragon was conquered through the power of Almighty God. If they would be converted and believe in God, George would finish off the wounded monster.

It was done. The king and people were converted, and George baptized them then and there. Then, with a mighty blow of his sword, he struck off the dragon's head, and there was an end to the terror.

The king offered George gold and silver, but George disdained these, saying they should be given to the poor. Instead, he made the king promise to build a church on the spot where the dragon had fallen.

Then George mounted his horse and rode away.

Painting from the Guild Chapel, Stratford-upon-Avon

*Write your own ballad of Saint George. Set a tune to it and sing it. Make a play based on the story of Saint George and the Dragon and tape-record it.*

# William Shakespeare

Shakespeare's coat of arms

William Shakespeare, England's greatest poet and dramatist, was probably born on St George's Day, 23 April, 1564, and may have died on the same date fifty-two years later in 1616.

"He was a handsome, well-shap't man: very good company, and of a very ready and pleasant smoothe wit," says John Aubrey in his *Brief Lives*.

In Stratford-upon-Avon, where Shakespeare was born and died, you can still see his birthplace, as well as the cottage his mother, Mary Arden, had lived in, his wife Anne Hathaway's cottage, and the house of his daughter and son-in-law, Hall's Croft.

Probably more has been written about the life and work of Shakespeare than any other single man. See what you can find out about him to make your own wall display. You might start by looking at Aubrey's account in *Brief Lives*. According to Aubrey, "This William, being inclined naturally to Poetry and acting, came to London, I guesse about 18: and was an Actor at one of the Playhouses, and did acte exceedingly well."

In London Shakespeare probably met and knew many of the famous men of the late Elizabethan age. He became a very successful playwright and theatre manager. He acquired a coat of arms, and a large house, called New Place, back at his home town of Stratford, which he was able to retire to before he was fifty.

When he died, a monument was set up in Stratford church, which can still be seen, and on his grave were set these words:

Good frend for Iesvs sake forbeare
To digg the dvst encloased heare:
Bleste be ye man yt spares thes stones,
And cvrst be he yt moves my bones.

MR. WILLIAM
SHAKESPEARES
COMEDIES,
HISTORIES, &
TRAGEDIES.
Publiſhed according to the True Originall Copies.

LONDON
Printed by Iſaac Iaggard, and Ed. Blount. 1623.

Title page of the First Folio edition of Shakespeare's plays

A drawing of the Swan Theatre made in 1596 when Shakespeare was writing his plays. It is the only drawing made inside an Elizabethan playhouse which still survives.

# Robin Hood

## The Bold Pedlar and Robin Hood

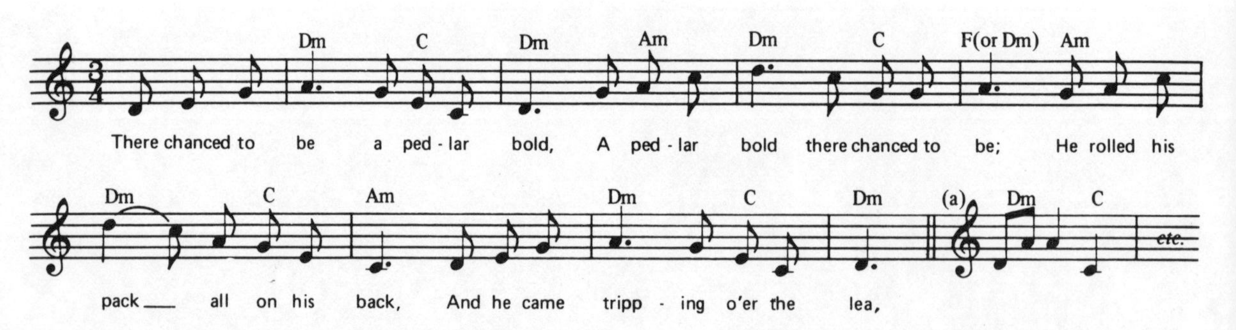


By chance he met two troublesome blades,
Two troublesome blades they chanced to be;
The one of them was bold Robin Hood,
And the other was little John, so free.

"Oh, pedlar, what is in thy pack?
Come speedily and tell to me".
"I've several suits of gay green silks
And silken bowstrings, two or three".

"If you've several suits of gay green silk
And silken bowstrings, two or three,
Then, by my body", cries little John,
"One half your pack belongs to me".

"Oh, nay, oh, nay", says the pedlar bold,
"Oh, nay, oh, nay, that cannot be;
There's never a man from fair Nottingham
Can take one half my pack from me".

The pedlar he pulled off his pack,
Put it a little below his knee,
Saying, "You move me one perch from this,
My pack and all shall gang with thee".

Then little John he drew his sword;
The pedlar by his pack did stand;
They fought until they both did sweat,
Till John cried, "Pedlar, pray hold your hand".

Then Robin Hood was standing by,
And he did laugh most heartily,
Saying, "I know a man of smaller scale
Could thrash the pedlar, and also thee".

"Go, you try, master", says little John,
"Go, you try, master, most speedily;
Or by my body", says little John,
"I'm sure this night you'll not know me".

Then Robin Hood he drew his sword,
And the pedlar by his pack did stand;
They fought till blood in streams did flow,
Till he cried, "Pedlar, pray hold your hand".

"Pedlar, pedlar, what is thy name?
Come speedily and tell to me".
"My name, my name, I ne'er will tell,
Till both your names you've told to me".

"The one of us is bold Robin Hood,
The other little John, so free".
"Now", says the pedlar, "it's my good will
Whether my name I tell to thee.

"I'm Gamble Gold of the gay green woods,
I've travelled far beyond the sea;
For killing a man in my father's land,
From my country I was forced to flee".

"If you're Gamble Gold of the gay green woods,
And travelled far beyond the sea,
You are my mother's own sister's son;
What nearer cousins then can we be?"

They sheathed their swords with friendly words,
So merrily they did agree;
They went to a tavern and there they dined,
And bottles cracked most merrily.

words adapted from *Ancient Poems*, 1846, by J. H. Dixon;
tune collected by Ralph Vaughan Williams and published in
*English Folk Song: Some Conclusions*, 1964, by Cecil Sharp

*Try xylophone accompaniment. During the first and last verses the chords could be broken into the rhythm indicated at (a). Verses with dialogue sung by solo voice or small groups should be lightly accompanied.*

*This might seem a long ballad, but some Robin Hood ballads have as many as 300 verses. There are a few unusual words here. "Perch" (verse 6) is an old measurement, still occasionally heard in the expression "one rod, pole or perch" (five-and-a-half yards). In the same verse, "gang" means "go". What do you think cracking bottles means in the last verse? Why do you think Nottingham is mentioned (verse 5)?*

*You might like to act out this story, and to make a frieze depicting it. Do you know any other songs or tales of Robin Hood and his men?*

# May Day

The first of May has always been a day associated with the coming of new life in the spring. In many parts of the country young girls get up early on May morning to wash their faces in the dew – they believe this will give them a good complexion throughout the coming year. In some parts of the British Isles, mainly the north and east, jokes and tricks, like those of April Fools' Day, are played, and the victim is known as a "May gosling" (or goose).

*Today 1 May is also known as Labour Day – what can you find out about it?*

## Cottesmore May Song

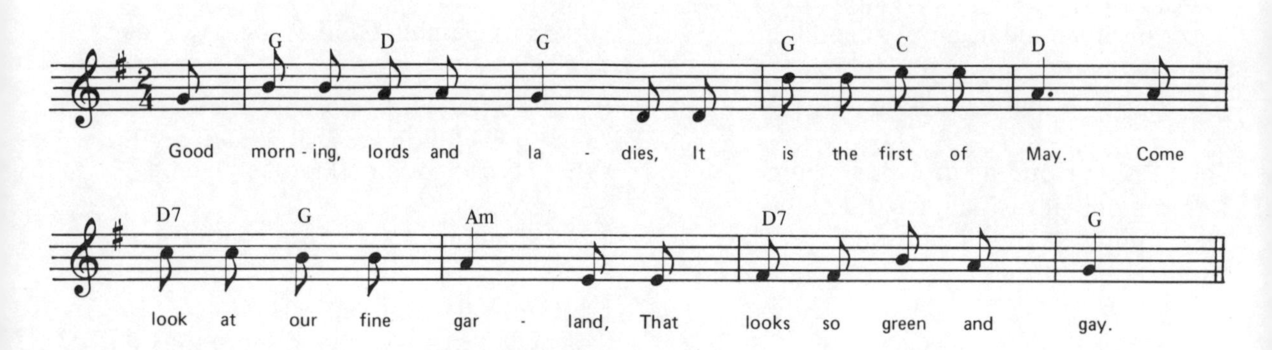


The cuckoo sings in April,
The cuckoo sings in May;
The cuckoo sings in June, July,
And then she flies away.

The cuckoo is a merry bird,
She sings as she flies.
She brings us good tidings,
And never tells no lies.

Traditional, from *May-day Songs and Celebrations in Leicestershire and Rutland* by Elizabeth Ruddock, in *Transactions of the Leicestershire Archaeological and Historical Society*, vol. XL, 1964–5

*This is an excellent processional song and, if used as such, is better sung without harmonic accompaniment. Instead, recorder or violin in unison with voices is effective, and/or a simple rhythmic ostinato on drum.*

Cottesmore was in the smallest county of England, Rutland. This no longer officially exists, but is part of Leicestershire.

## Bringing in the May

The ceremony of "bringing in the May" is centuries old. In 1648, Robert Herrick wrote:

> There's not a budding Boy or Girl, this day,
> But is got up and gone to bring in May.

The young people used to get up early and go into the woods to fetch armfuls of May blossom to decorate the maypole.

The maypole was a tall tree set up by itself on the green. All its branches were cut off, and it became the centrepiece for the day's festivities and celebrations. Round the maypole, dancing, games, plays and tests of strength took place. It was all part of an ancient fertility cult, and some people believed that because it was old and un-Christian, it should be stopped. One such was Philip Stubbes, who wrote about the maypole in Elizabethan times:

But their chiefest jewel they bring from thence is their maypole, which they bring home with great veneration, as thus: They have twenty or forty yoke of oxen, every ox having a sweet nosegay of flowers tied on the tip of his horns, and these oxen draw home this maypole (this stinking idol rather), which is covered all over with flowers and herbs, bound about with strings, from the top to the bottom, and sometimes painted with variable colours, with two or three hundred men, women and children following it, with great devotion. And thus being reared up, with handkerchiefs and flags streaming at the top, they strew the ground about, bind green boughs about it, set up summer halls, bowers and arbours hard by it. And then they fall to banquet and feast, to leap and dance about it, as the heathen people did, at the dedication of their idols, whereof this is a perfect pattern, or rather the thing itself.

Raising the maypole

Northampton May garland

## May Day at Lark Rise

The garland was made, or "dressed", in the school-room. . . . The foundation of the garland was a light wooden framework of uprights supporting graduated hoops, forming a bell-shaped structure about four feet high. This frame was covered with flowers, bunched and set closely, after the manner of wreath-making.

On the last morning of April the children would come to school with bunches, baskets, arms and pinafores full of flowers – every blossom they could find in the fields and hedges or beg from parents and neighbours. . . .

Piled on desks, table, and floor, this supply appeared inexhaustible; but the garland was large, and as the work of dressing it proceeded, it soon became plain that the present stock wouldn't "hardly go nowheres," as the children said. So foraging parties were sent out, one to the Rectory, another to Squire's, and others to outlying farm-houses and cottages. All returned loaded, and in time the wooden frame was covered. . . . The fragrant, bowering structure was sprinkled with water and set aside for the night.

While the garland was being dressed, an older girl, perhaps the May Queen herself, would be busy in a corner making the crown. This always had to be a daisy crown; garden daisies, white and red, were used, with a background of dark, glossy, evergreen leaves.

* * *

The final touches were given the garland when the children assembled at six o'clock on May Day morning. Then a large china doll in a blue frock was brought forth from the depths of the school needlework chest and arranged in a sitting position on a little ledge in the centre front of the garland. This doll was known as "the lady," and a doll of some kind was considered essential. Even in those parishes where the garland had degenerated into a shabby nosegay carried aloft at the top of a stick, some dollish image was mixed in with the flowers. The attitude of the children to the lady is interesting. It was understood that the garland was her garland, carried in her honour. The lady must never be roughly handled. If the garland turned turtle, as it was apt to do late in the day, when the road was rough and the bearers were growing weary, the first question was always, "Is the lady all right?"

* * *

All the children in the parish between the ages of seven and eleven were by this time assembled as follows:

Boy with flag. Girl with money-box.

THE GARLAND with two bearers.

King and queen.

Two maids of honour.

Lord and Lady.

Two maids of honour.

Footman and footman's lady.

Rank and file, walking in twos.

Girl known as "Mother". Boy called "Ragman".

The "Mother" was one of the most dependable of the older girls, who was made responsible for the behaviour of the garlanders. She carried a large, old-fashioned, double-lidded marketing basket over her arm, containing the lunches of the principal actors. The boy called "Ragman" carried the coats, brought in case of rain, but seldom worn, even during a shower, lest by their poverty and shabbiness they should disgrace the festive attire.

The procession stepped out briskly. Mothers waved and implored their offspring to behave well; some of the little ones left behind lifted up their voices and wept; old people came to cottage gates and said that, though well enough, this year's procession was poor compared to some they had seen. But the garlanders paid no heed; they had their feet on the road at last and vowed they would not turn back now, "not if it rained cats and dogs."

The first stop was at the Rectory, where the garland was planted before the front door and the shrill little voices struck up, shyly at first, but gathering confidence as they went on:

A bunch of may I have brought you
   And at your door it stands.
It is but a sprout, but it's well put about
   By the Lord Almighty's hands.

God bless the master of this house
   God bless the mistress too,
And all the little children
   That round the table go.

And now I've sung my short little song
   I must no longer stay.
God bless you all, both great and small,
   And send you a happy May Day.

During the singing of this the Rector's face, wearing its mildest expression, and bedaubed with shaving lather, for it was only as yet seven o'clock, would appear at an upper window and nod approval and admiration of the garland. His daughter would be down and at the door, and for her the veil was lifted and the glory of the garland revealed. She would look, touch and smell, then slip a silver coin into the money-box, and the procession would move on towards Squire's. . .

After becoming duty had been paid to the Big House, the farm-house and cottages were visited; then the little procession set out along narrow, winding country roads, with tall hedges of blackthorn and bursting leaf-buds on either side, to make its seven-mile circuit. In those days there were no motors to dodge and there was very little other traffic; just a farm cart here and there, or the baker's white-tilted van, or a governess car with nurses and children out for their airing. Sometimes the garlanders would forsake the road for stiles and footpaths across buttercup meadows or go through parks and gardens to call at some big house or secluded farmstead.

* * *

There came a point in the circuit when faces were turned towards home, instead of away from it; and at last, at long last, the lights in the Lark Hill windows shone clear through the spring twilight. The great day was over, for ever, as it seemed, for at ten years old a year seems as long as a century. Still, there was the May money to be shared out in school the next morning, and the lady to be stroked before being put back in her box, and the flowers which had survived to be put in water: even tomorrow would not be quite a common day. So the last waking thoughts blended with dreams of swans and peacocks and footmen and sore feet and fat cooks with pink faces wearing daisy crowns which turned into pure gold, then melted away.

adapted from *Lark Rise to Candleford* by Flora Thompson

## Nuts in May

Nowadays May flowers are not always out by 1 May, but before the calendar was changed in 1752 May Day fell eleven days later and garlands of May flowers were much more likely to be in their full bloom. The little children's game, "Here We Come Gathering Nuts in May", seems an odd title because there are no nuts at that time of the year. It should really be *knots* in May, a reference to the knotted May garlands that used to be gathered.

### May Rhymes

Marry in May
Rue for aye.

A wet May
Makes big loads of hay.

Milk Maids Dancing on May-day.

## Jack-in-the-Green

Jack-in-the-Green, or the Green Man, is a figure from medieval May Day celebrations. Sometimes he was covered in greenery from head to foot and came out of the forest to represent the coming of spring. Sometimes he was a man shut up in a big wooden box covered with greenery, and he was let out of this to dance with the May Queen, again representing the coming of spring.

Today, the Green Man is often the name of a pub, and sometimes Jack-in-the-Green is shown on the inn sign. In some old churches there are carvings of him, with leaves and greenery growing out of his mouth, as in the one shown on this page.

A roof-boss with a carving of Jack-in-the-Green from Worcester Cathedral

## *The Green Knight*

*Jack-in-the-Green is related to the Green Knight in the story of* Sir Gawain and the Green Knight. *This story makes an excellent subject for your own play, and a particularly good telling of it is in* The Hamish Hamilton Book of Myths and Legends *by Jacynth Hope-Simpson (H. Hamilton, 1964).*

## Jack-in-the-Green in London, 1887

It was on the first of May that I had one of the frights of my life. I was playing alone in the Terrace garden when I heard the jingling of bells and went to the end of the garden to investigate. A motley group of men rigged up for "Jack-in-the-Green" was turning into the Terrace. One fellow, completely covered with greenery, so that only his legs were showing, was jigging up and down. Another had his face smeared with paint to represent a clown, and a third, in striped cloth coat and trousers, with a huge collar and a blackened face, was beating a tambourine. But the one that really frightened me was a man got up as a woman, in a coloured, ill-fitting dress, a wig made of tow, and showing brawny arms above dirty white gloves. Brandishing a tattered parasol, he, or she, held it out to catch coins thrown by passers-by or from the houses. Fascinated, I watched their progress from behind the bushes. Then I made a bolt for home. But I had left it too late. As I emerged from the gate the man-woman spotted me and came prancing up, calling out, "What have you got for Jack-in-th'-Green, little gentleman?" Petrified with fear, I ran back into the garden, and made for the sloping tree we always climbed. I was up it in a jiffy, but the dreadful creature, grinning like a satyr, followed me into the garden and started to dance around, while the others clattered and banged and shouted encouragement from the gateway.

'Jack-in-the-Green'

I was fast losing my reason when a welcome face appeared at the area steps – it was Lizzie. She took in the situation at a glance and up she came. Her indignation was more for the state of my clothes than anything else, but the enemy gave way before her and, blowing kisses and still dancing, the troupe passed on. I must have been almost hysterical when I was taken in and washed, and I never could bear the sight of a man dressed as a woman after that.

from *Drawn from Memory* by E. H. Shepard

## Northamptonshire May Song

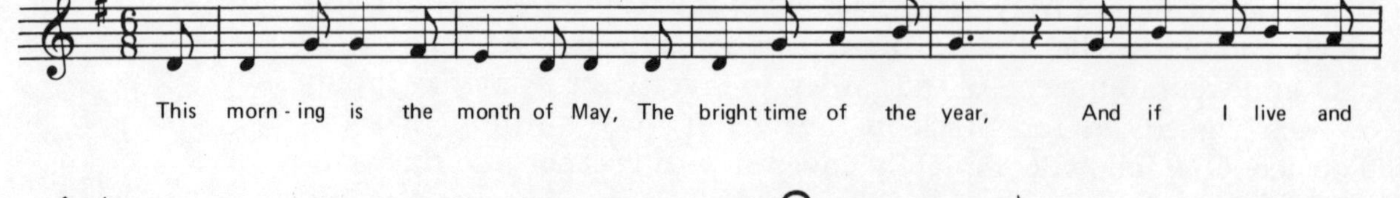

The fields and meadows are so green,
As green as any leaf;
Our Heavenly Father waters them,
With his heavenly dew so sweet.

A man, a man, his life's a span,
He flourishes like a flower;
He's here today and gone tomorrow,
He's gone in one short hour.

The clock strikes one, I must be gone,
I can no longer stay,
So come downstairs, my pretty maids all,
And look at my bunch of May.

A branch of May I've brought you here,
Before your door it stands;
It's well set out and spread about,
It's the work of our Lord's hand.

So take a Bible in your hand
And read a chapter through,
So when the day of judgement comes
God will remember you.

I have a purse all in my pocket,
It's drawn with a silken string,
And all it wants is a little money
To line it well within.

from *Green Groves: More English Folk Songs*, 1973, ed. by F. Hamer

*A circular tune, better not harmonized. Try unison recorder and drum accompaniment.*

Cowslips

Come queen of months in company
With all thy merry minstrelsy
The restless cuckoo absent long
And twittering swallows chimney song
And hedge-row crickets notes that run
From every bank that fronts the sun
And swathy bees about the grass
That stops with every bloom they pass
And every minute every hour
Keep teazing weeds that wear a flower
And toil and childhood's humming joys
For there is music in the noise
The village children mad for sport
In school times leisure ever short
That crick and catch the bouncing ball
And run along the church yard wall
Capped with rude figured slabs whose claims
In times bad memory hath no names
Oft racing round the nooky church
Or calling echoes in the porch
And jilting o'er the weather cock
Viewing with jealous eyes the clock
Oft leaping grave stones leaning heights
Uncheck'd with melancholy sights
The green grass swell'd in many a heap
Where kin and friends and parents sleep
Unthinking in their jovial cry
That time shall come when they shall lye
As lowly and as still as they
While other boys above them play
Heedless as they do now to know
The unconscious dust that lies below.

from *The Shepherd's Calendar* by John Clare

# Inn Signs

*"The Green Man," which is mentioned on page 48, is an inn sign which is very old. Ever since there have been inns or pubs, they have displayed signs to attract customers, and many common names of pubs go back several centuries. For instance, the "Vine" and "Bush" are signs which were probably brought to this country by the Romans: the vine or bush was the symbol of Bacchus, the Roman god of wine.*

*Today there are many types of sign, often beautifully drawn and attractively coloured. For example, there are signs depicting royalty and coats of arms, signs of animals, birds, trees and flowers, signs of railways and canals, and signs commemorating great events or people from the past.*

*An interesting project is to make a survey of the inn signs in the district you live in. List the names and say whether each has a pictorial sign. Photograph any interesting signs. On a map, mark where each pub is. Try to find out how each one got its name – the first way of trying to find this out is to write to the brewery whose beer the pub serves. You could mount the results of your project on the wall as a display.*

*Many pubs are worth looking at as buildings. They are often older than the houses round them and sometimes have eye-catching frontages or are painted in gaudy colours to attract the passer-by. Draw or photograph the front of an interesting pub to add to your display.*

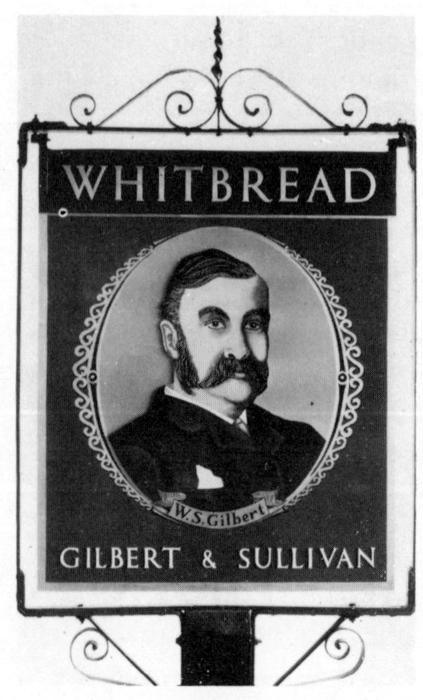

# Gravestones

*The May song and May poem on pages 50 and 51 celebrate the coming of new life in spring, but they also remind us that what is born has to die.*

*In many churchyards you can see interesting and unusual memorials to those who have died. Many gravestones are beautifully made and show fine craftsmanship in the lettering, sculpture and often the use of local stone. They are a record of how people have lived, what they have believed and what has been important in their lives. They tell us of the trades and businesses of our ancestors, and sometimes of how they spent their leisure time.*

*Do a survey of your local churchyard. On a graph, show how many burials there were in each year. Find out if there is a reason why there might have been more deaths in one year than another – for instance was there some sort of epidemic in that year? Are there any people whom you could find out more about – a sportsman, a trade union official, a criminal? Take photographs of any interesting gravestones, and copy out any unusual inscriptions – some may be funny, some pathetic, some frightening, reminding us of our own death. A good book on this subject is* Discovering Epitaphs *by G. N. Wright (Shire Publications), which contains photographs of some of the oddest gravestones in the country.*

*You might like to try writing some epitaphs, either for imaginary people or for people that you know. Here are two comic epitaphs to start with:*

Here lies a man who was killed by lightning;
He died when his prospects seemed to be brightening.
He might have cut a flash in this world of trouble,
But the flash cut him, and he lies in the stubble.

Here lies a mother of twenty-eight;
It might have been more but now
it's too late.

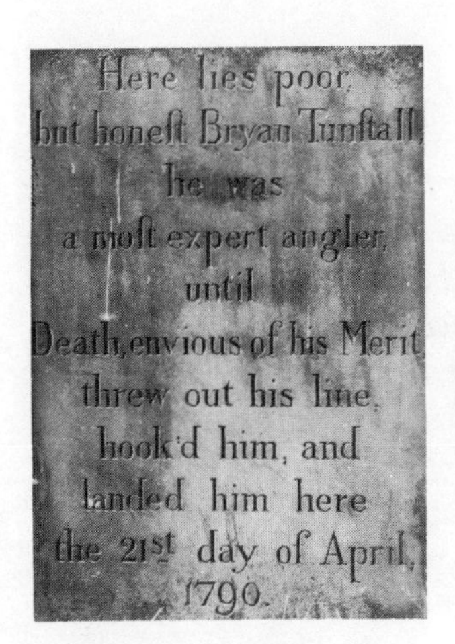

A gardener's headstone

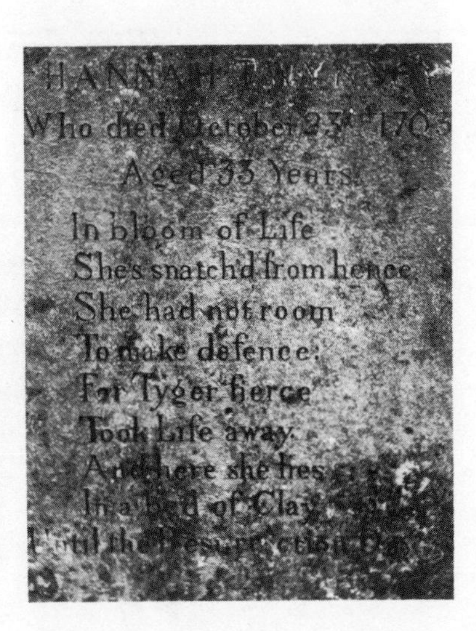

# Morris Dancing

May Day was one of the occasions when morris dancers came out, as was Whit Monday (now Spring Bank Holiday Monday, usually falling in the last week of May). The Cotswold Morris has six dancers, usually dressed in white, wearing coloured sashes, and having bells and ribbons fastened to their legs. They wave handkerchieves or clash sticks, and often have a clown – sometimes a man dressed up as a woman.

You can read not only about morris, but other dances in Hugh Rippon's book, *Discovering English Folk Dance,* Shire Publications, 1975.

## *The Gisburn Processional*

*This is danced by a team of twelve men and twelve women annually at the Village Field Day, at Gisburn, Lancashire. The men wear white shirts, red knee breeches, white stockings, yellow sashes, red ties and clogs, and have bells fastened to their breeches at the knees. The women wear white dresses, red sashes over the left shoulder tied on the right hip, with bells across the chest, red stockings and clogs, and a red band on their hair.*

*All carry short white sticks with a bell attached at each end, the men's wound round with red braid and the women's with yellow braid. These sticks are carried in the outside hand by their sides during the procession and at head level during the dancing of the figures, and continuously shaken to ring the bells. The dance is done throughout with the left foot leading, a jaunty walking step for the procession, skipping step for the figures.*

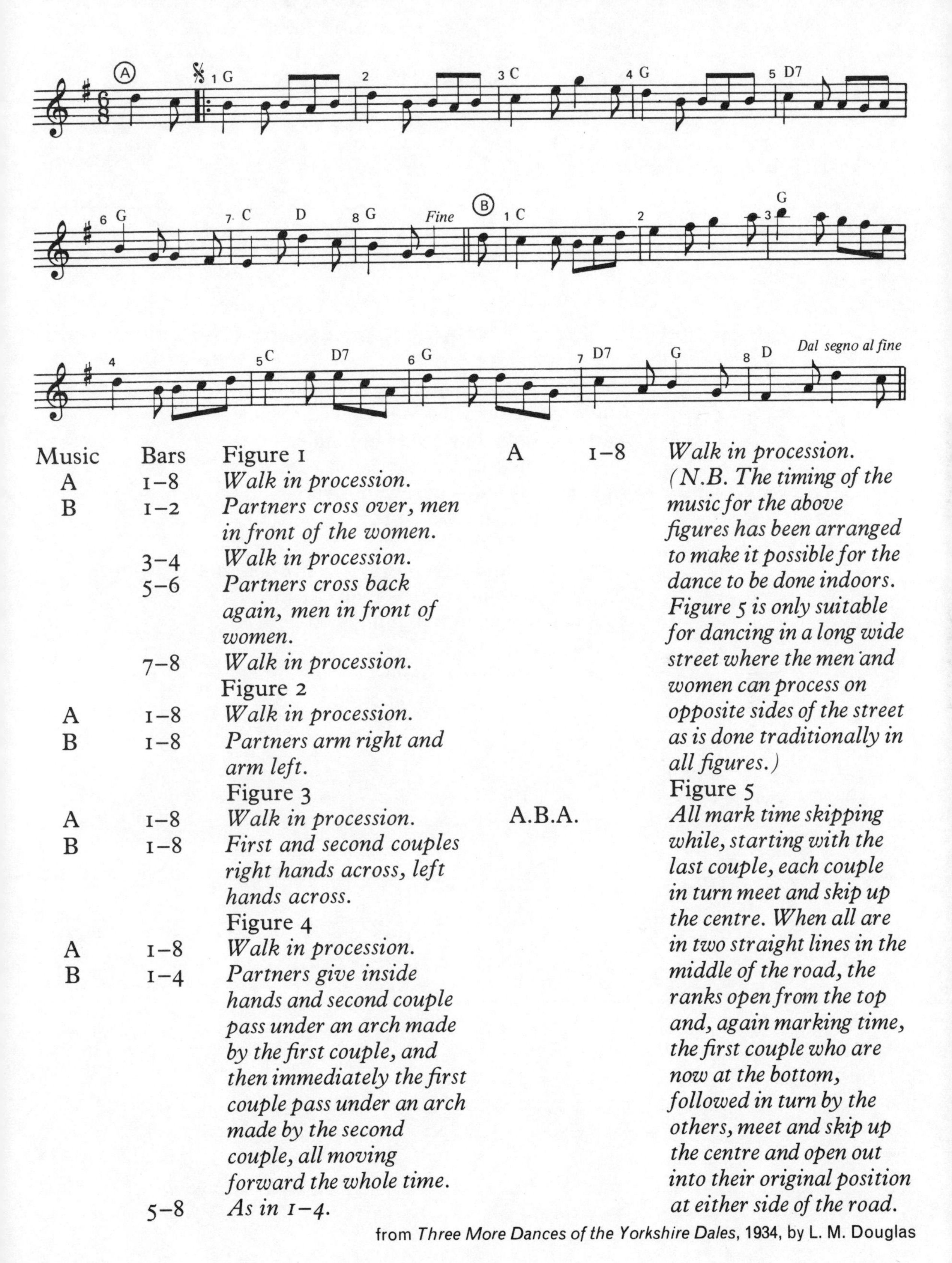


| Music | Bars | |
|---|---|---|
| | | Figure 1 |
| A | 1–8 | *Walk in procession.* |
| B | 1–2 | *Partners cross over, men in front of the women.* |
| | 3–4 | *Walk in procession.* |
| | 5–6 | *Partners cross back again, men in front of women.* |
| | 7–8 | *Walk in procession.* |
| | | Figure 2 |
| A | 1–8 | *Walk in procession.* |
| B | 1–8 | *Partners arm right and arm left.* |
| | | Figure 3 |
| A | 1–8 | *Walk in procession.* |
| B | 1–8 | *First and second couples right hands across, left hands across.* |
| | | Figure 4 |
| A | 1–8 | *Walk in procession.* |
| B | 1–4 | *Partners give inside hands and second couple pass under an arch made by the first couple, and then immediately the first couple pass under an arch made by the second couple, all moving forward the whole time.* |
| | 5–8 | *As in 1–4.* |
| A | 1–8 | *Walk in procession. (N.B. The timing of the music for the above figures has been arranged to make it possible for the dance to be done indoors. Figure 5 is only suitable for dancing in a long wide street where the men and women can process on opposite sides of the street as is done traditionally in all figures.)* |
| | | Figure 5 |
| A.B.A. | | *All mark time skipping while, starting with the last couple, each couple in turn meet and skip up the centre. When all are in two straight lines in the middle of the road, the ranks open from the top and, again marking time, the first couple who are now at the bottom, followed in turn by the others, meet and skip up the centre and open out into their original position at either side of the road.* |

from *Three More Dances of the Yorkshire Dales*, 1934, by L. M. Douglas

## Proud Songsters

The thrushes sing as the sun is going,
And the finches whistle in ones and pairs,
And as it gets dark loud nightingales
    In bushes
Pipe, as they can when April wears,
    As if all Time were theirs.

These are brand-new birds of twelve-months' growing,
Which a year ago, or less than twain
No finches were, nor nightingales,
    Nor thrushes,
But only particles of grain,
    And earth, and air, and rain.

Thomas Hardy

# Reference Section for Teachers

*Books*

A useful source of general reference about folk customs and practices is *Folklore, Myth and Legends of Britain*, published by the Readers' Digest Association. Geoffrey Palmer and Noel Lloyd's *A Year of Festivals* (Frederick Warne) is also a comprehensive guide to British calendar customs and is a useful library book. See also *The Country Life Book of Old English Customs* by Roy Christian (Country Life).

A number of the books in the "Discovering" series published by Shire Publications, Tring, Herts. are also useful. Some of these have been mentioned in the text, and we would particularly recommend Margaret Gascoigne's *Discovering English Customs and Traditions*, and *Discovering English Folk Dance* by Hugh Rippon. There are numerous books dealing in detail with the folklore of different parts of the British Isles. The major publishing houses dealing in such matters include Batsford, David and Charles, E. P. Publishing, and Routledge and Kegan Paul. It is worthwhile consulting their catalogues to see if they have published any books dealing specifically with your own locality. Bob Copper's *A Song for Every Season* (Heinemann) will also be a valuable addition to the library resources. Other useful books are *The Jarrold Book of the Countryside in Spring* (Jarrold), *Nature Through the Seasons* by Richard Adams and Max Hooper (Kestrel Books) and *An Egg at Easter* by Venetia Newell (Routledge).

The Robin Hood ballads were first collected in *Robin Hood*, edited by J. Ritson, and published in 1795. A facsimile reprint of the 1823 edition was published in 1972 by E. P. Publishing, Wakefield.

*Records*

The major folk song record company is Topic Records of 27 Nassington Road, London NW3 2TX. Their complete catalogue is well worth having, especially as it lists several collections of local folk songs belonging to particular areas of the British Isles. We would especially recommend the Watersons' records, including *Frost and Fire* (12T 136). Two other Topic records are also very useful, but it should be noted that they consist of field recordings of elderly singers, and may not always be easy to use with younger pupils. They are *Songs of Ceremony* (12T 197) and *Songs of Animals and Other Marvels* (12T 198). There is also a record (LED 2067) based on the book, *A Song for Every Season*, produced by Leader Records, 209 Rochdale Road, Halifax, Yorks., HX4 8SE.

*Film*

Rank Film Library, 1 Aintree Road, Perivale, Greenford, Middlesex, have a film about Jack-in-the-Green in their *Look at Life* series.

*Kit*

There are many books, filmstrips, records, etc. which are useful for further work on Shakespeare. An interesting kit which contains workcards, illustrated material, filmstrip, record and teacher's handbook is *Shakespeare's England*, a Beaver Unit by Joy Thwaytes (George Philip & Son Ltd).

*Museums and Libraries*

There are an increasing number of museums with local folklore collections and also several local specialist folk museums. Full details of all these will be found in the annual A.B.C. Publication, *A Guide to Museums and Art Galleries in Great Britain*, which is a very helpful source of information.

Most libraries also have a local collection of great interest.

*Organizations*

The following national organizations can provide much help and information:

The English Folk Dance and Song Society whose headquarters are at Cecil Sharp House, 2 Regent's Park Road, London NW1 7AY. The Society publishes an annual Folk Directory which gives up-to-date information about folk-customs, and there is also the Ralph Vaughan Williams Memorial Library at Cecil Sharp House itself. This includes a useful picture collection.

The Folklore Society, c/o University College, Gower Street, London WC1E 6BT can also provide help and information.

In addition, there are numerous local history and archaeological societies that can provide speakers or mount exhibitions in schools. Many of these produce local publications of great value for teaching purposes.